KIDS SPEAK OUT *About*

INEQUALITY

#INCLUDE

MAKE A CHANGE!

Celebrate Differences! #EMPOWER

 EQUAL OPPORTUNITY

KIDS CARE!

#FAIR

#chance

CHRIS SCHWAB

Rourke
Educational Media

A Division of
Carson
Dellosa
Education

BEFORE AND DURING READING ACTIVITIES

Before Reading: *Building Background Knowledge and Vocabulary*

Building background knowledge can help children process new information and build upon what they already know. Before reading a book, it is important to tap into what children already know about the topic. This will help them develop their vocabulary and increase their reading comprehension.

Questions and Activities to Build Background Knowledge:

1. Look at the front cover of the book and read the title. What do you think this book will be about?
2. What do you already know about this topic?
3. Take a book walk and skim the pages. Look at the table of contents, photographs, captions, and bold words. Did these text features give you any information or predictions about what you will read in this book?

Vocabulary: *Vocabulary Is Key to Reading Comprehension*

Use the following directions to prompt a conversation about each word.

- Read the vocabulary words.
- What comes to mind when you see each word?
- What do you think each word means?

> ## Vocabulary Words:
> - *discrimination*
> - *documentary*
> - *gender*
> - *Indigenous*
> - *protest*
> - *representation*
> - *social media*
> - *transgender*

During Reading: *Reading for Meaning and Understanding*

To achieve deep comprehension of a book, children are encouraged to use close reading strategies. During reading, it is important to have children stop and make connections. These connections result in deeper analysis and understanding of a book.

 Close Reading a Text

During reading, have children stop and talk about the following:

- Any confusing parts
- Any unknown words
- Text to text, text to self, text to world connections
- The main idea in each chapter or heading

Encourage children to use context clues to determine the meaning of any unknown words. These strategies will help children learn to analyze the text more thoroughly as they read.

When you are finished reading this book, turn to the next-to-last page for **Text-Dependent Questions** and an **Extension Activity**.

Table of Contents

What Is Inequality?

Inequality is when one person gets better opportunities or is treated better than another. Another word for inequality is **discrimination**. The reasons for inequality are always bad. It could be because of someone's race. It could be because of someone's **gender**. It could be because someone is poor.

Inequality is never fair. One kid eats big meals, another kid is hungry. One kid is popular, another kid is bullied. Examples are all around us.

Racial Inequality

Is it fair that the color of your skin can decide how you are treated? If someone likes you or not? If you have a chance at a job you want? No, it isn't fair! This is called racial inequality.

The United States has a long history of racial inequality. People of many different races are Americans, but they are not always treated the same. The Civil Rights Movement, which happened in the 1950s and 1960s, tried to change that. During this time, people marched and protested for the rights of African Americans.

Dr. Martin Luther King Jr. gave his famous "I Have a Dream" speech to a huge crowd in Washington, DC, in 1963.

Dr. Martin Luther King Jr.

Freeman A. Hrabowski III was only 12 years old when he heard Dr. King speak at his church. He spoke about a plan for a peaceful **protest**. Freeman knew he wanted to be part of the protest.

Freeman's parents didn't know if they should let him go. They were scared! It was dangerous for an African American kid. But they decided to let him go. At the protest, Freeman was arrested and sent to jail for five days. He wasn't allowed to see his parents. He focused on lifting the spirits of the other kids arrested with him.

Dr. King visited the kids while they were in jail. He said, "What you do this day will have an impact on children yet unborn." Freeman always remembered that!

Freeman A. Hrabowski III

Fast Forward

Freeman loved learning. When he grew up, he became a mathematician and the president of a college. He never stopped working for equality. He made it his mission to encourage more African American kids to get into math and science.

Our race is an important and good part of who we are. We want to see people who look like us on TV, at the movies, and in books. When we don't see people who look like us, it is a problem of **representation**.

Eleven-year-old Marley Dias noticed she was reading a lot of books about white boys in school. Marley wanted to read books about black girls like her! She decided to speak out about this inequality.

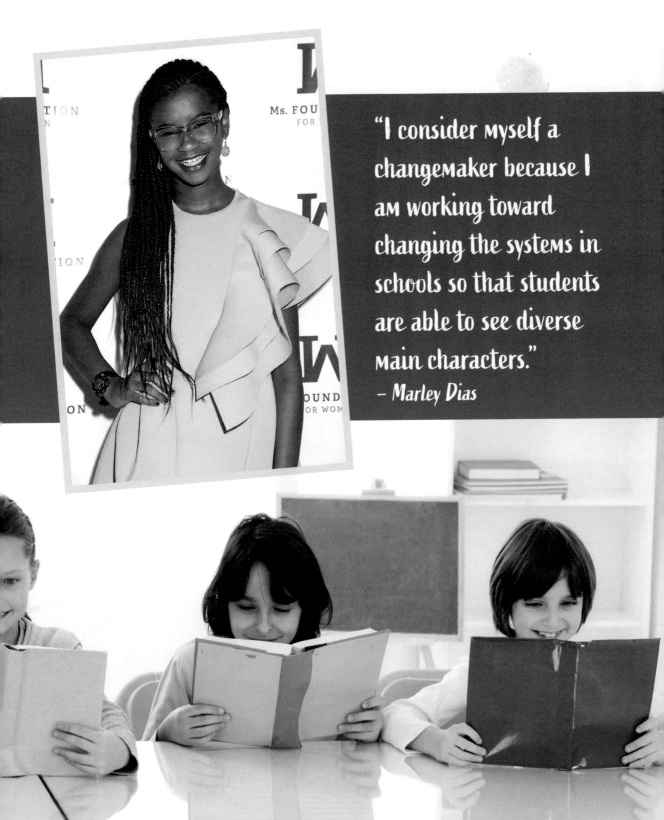

"I consider myself a changemaker because I am working toward changing the systems in schools so that students are able to see diverse main characters."
— Marley Dias

Marley Dias

Marley wanted to live in a world where black girls are represented. So she started a **social media** project called #1000BlackGirlBooks. Her plan was to find and donate 1,000 books that put the spotlight on black girls. She ended up donating over 12,000 books!

Marley Gets It Done!

Marley doesn't just read books. She's written one! Her book *Marley Dias Gets It Done: And So Can You!* came out in 2018. In it, she talks about making the world a better place. Marley tells kids how to make their dreams come true!

Gender Inequality

In some parts of the world, girls face different problems than boys. One of these places is Concepción Chiquirichapa, Guatemala. Most of the people in Concepción Chiquirichapa are Maya Mam, an **Indigenous** group. Many of the girls there have responsibilities at home that make it hard to stay in school. Very few of these girls finish high school.

When she was 13 years old, Emelin Cabrera asked the mayor of Concepción Chiquirichapa to do something to help girls stay in school. He told her she was wasting his time. Emelin didn't give up. When the Let Girls Lead program came to town, Emelin got the opportunity she needed.

Let Girls Lead

Let Girls Lead is a program for girls ages 10 to 19. It teaches them how to use their voices to stand up for themselves and make a change.

Emelin Cabrera

Emelin learned how to make her voice heard. She and her friend Elba were interviewed for the newspaper. Their message was talked about on TV and on the radio. The mayor heard them and changed his mind. He signed laws to help provide education and health care for girls.

¡PODER!

The word *poder* is Spanish for "power." It is the title of a **documentary** made about Emelin's story. Emelin and Elba star in it. They hope their story will inspire belief in the power of girls.

Sometimes who you are on the inside doesn't match what you look like on the outside. Body parts don't always make you a boy or a girl. You might identify with a different gender than what people think or have told you that you are. This would make you **transgender**.

People who are transgender often face inequality. They might be bullied. They might find that others refuse to call them by the name they want to be called. But everyone deserves to live life as the person they really are.

Jazz Jennings

Jazz Jennings was assigned the gender "boy" at birth. But Jazz always knew she was a girl. Jazz is transgender. She started sharing her story when she was only six years old. She's proud of who she is.

Jazz speaks out to help other transgender kids. She wants to spread a message of acceptance. She wants transgender people to feel safe and free to be who they are. She speaks out on social media, YouTube, and TV. Her TV show is called *I Am Jazz*. She also wrote a book titled *Being Jazz*.

What can you do when you see inequality? Speak out like Freeman, Marley, Emelin, Elba, and Jazz. Help change the world!

The transgender pride flag

TransKids Purple Rainbow Foundation (TKPRF)

TKPRF was started by Jazz and her parents to help transgender kids get equal rights in their schools. They want transgender kids to be safe and free from bullying. They ask parents and kids to support them.

Top 10 Ways to Get Involved

1 Learn! Seek out information about people who face inequality.

2 Share what you learn with friends or family.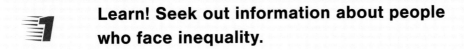

3 Think about your words. Make a change if they hurt others or cause inequality.

4 Be okay with being wrong. If you say something and are told it was hurtful, listen.

5 Speak out! If you hear someone using hurtful words, tell them you are not okay with that.

6 Start a savings jar to collect money. After a year, donate it to an organization that fights inequality.

7 Hold a bake sale. Donate the money to an organization that fights inequality.

8 Make friends with all kinds of people.

9 If you see someone being bullied because they are different in any way, tell an adult and make it stop.

10 Use the chosen names and pronouns of transgender people. If you don't know, ask.

Glossary

discrimination (diss-krim-uh-NAY-shuhn): prejudice or unfair treatment of others based on differences in things such as race or gender

documentary (dahk-yuh-MEN-tur-ee): a movie or TV program about real people and events

gender (JEN-dur): the behavioral and cultural characteristics typically associated with the male or female sex

Indigenous (in-DI-juh-nes): people who are originally from a particular place

protest (PROH-test): demonstration against something

representation (rep-ri-zen-TAY-shuhn): the act of being represented, especially in books, TV shows, and other types of media

social media (SOH-shuhl MEE-dee-uh): electronic communication, such as websites, where ideas, pictures, and messages are shared

transgender (trans-JEN-dur): referring to a person whose gender identity is different from what they were born with

Index

Text-Dependent Questions

1. Name a type of inequality.
2. What change did Emelin help make?
3. What is a sign that there is a problem of representation?
4. What might transgender kids face in their schools?
5. What do Freeman, Marley, Emelin, Elba, and Jazz have in common?

Extension Activity

You will need a paper plate and a pen or marker. On the outside of your paper plate, write something someone might think about you just from looking at you. On the inside, write some things that describe who you are on the inside. How would you feel if people only knew the outside of your plate? Think about what might be on other people's paper plates.

About the Author

Chris Schwab is a writer and editor. She has written many articles for newspapers and magazines. Now she writes books for kids. She also taught school in a number of places. Not all of the schools were equal. One school did not have any books! It was easy to see that children learn better when there are plenty of supplies.

Quote sources: Joseph Mosnier "Freeman Hrabowski Oral History Interview, Part 2," Southern Oral History Program, C-SPAN, July 14, 2011, https://www.c-span.org/video/?83852-101/freeman-hrabowski-oral-history-interview-part-2 ; Lara Deloza, "Marley Dias on Inspiring Activism, Diversifying Children's Literature, and Her Latest Reads," International Literacy Association, May 31, 2018, https://literacyworldwide.org/blog/literacy-daily/2018/05/31/marley-dias-on-inspiring-activism-diversifying-children's-literature-and-her-latest-reads

www.rourkeeducationalmedia.com

PHOTO CREDIT: Cover, p1 ©ronniechua, ©Nikada, ©calvindexter, ©Hulinska_©Yevhenila, ©Bubushonok, ©ulimi; p4 ©Hyejin Kang; p6 ©ertyo5; p7 ©Everett Historical; p8 ©files UPI Photo Service/Newscom; p9 ©Photo courtesy of the Hrabowski Family; p10 ©skynesherp16; p11 ©Robin Platzer/Twin Images/Avalon.red/Newscom; p12 ©Cheriss May/NurPhoto/TNS/Newscom; p13 ©tanuha2001; p14 ©Rodrigo García; p15 ©UN Photo/Mark Garten; p16 ©Byron Ortiz; p17 ©Kapitosh; p18-19 ©Jilll Richardson p20 ©lev radin, ©llewellyn_chin.

Edited by: Hailey Scragg
Cover and interior layout by: Kathy Walsh and Morgan Burnside

Library of Congress PCN Data

Kids Speak Out About Inequality / Chris Schwab
(Kids Speak Out)
ISBN 978-1-73163-858-8 (hard cover)(alk. paper)
ISBN 978-1-73163-935-6 (soft cover)
ISBN 978-1-73164-012-3 (e-Book)
ISBN 978-1-73164-089-5 (ePub)
Library of Congress Control Number: 2020930056

Rourke Educational Media
Printed in the United States of America
01-1942011937